Thank you very much for coming. It's wonderful to meet you at last.

Anne Ryland

Autumnologist

Anne Ryland

ARROWHEAD
PRESS

First published 2006 by
Arrowhead Press
70 Clifton Road, Darlington
Co. Durham, DL1 5DX
Tel: (01325) 260741

Typeset in 10 on 11pt Janson Text by
Arrowhead Press

Email: editor@arrowheadpress.co.uk
Website: http://www.arrowheadpress.co.uk

ISBN-10: 1-904852-11-4
ISBN-13: 978-1-904852-11-7

Arrowhead Press acknowledges the financial assistance of
Arts Council England, North East.

Arrowhead Press is a member of
Independent Northern Publishers.

Printed by Athenaeum Press, Gateshead, Tyne and Wear.

for David

and in memory of my mother

Acknowledgements

Thanks are due to the editors of the following where some of the poems in this book, or versions of them, first appeared:

Acumen; Brittle Star; Coffee House; Diamond Twig Poems of the Month; The Eildon Tree; Entering the Tapestry (Enitharmon, 2003); Envoi; Equinox; Four Caves of the Heart (Second Light, 2004); Franks Casket; The Frogmore Papers; The Interpreter's House; iota; London Magazine; Magma; Making Worlds (Headland, 2003); Miracle and Clockwork (Other Poetry Editions, 2005); Northwords; Orbis; Other Poetry; Quattrocento; The Red Wheelbarrow; Scintilla; Seam; Smiths Knoll; Staple.

I would like to thank all those who have offered invaluable guidance with these poems. Special thanks are due to Moniza Alvi and Pascale Petit for their perceptive comments and ongoing encouragement.

Anne Ryland

Cover Image:
'Inverdovat Pond'
Acrylic 14"x 14"
© Deborah Phillips BA(Hons) 2006

Contents

Listening for Winter

That it will never come again is what makes life so sweet.
Emily Dickinson

Dusk will never be such apricot and violet again
neither will its layers bleed together
so fluently. The river will darken down
for the night, folding over a different story,
cradling another moon at a precise slant
not to be repeated. The windows will smear
with a fresh storm pattern and these stone walls
will grow restless, holding still more of the past.
The blue inside me will lighten or deepen,
the ice in my hands will melt or shatter.
The quiet will not be the same quiet.
Never again will I listen this closely for winter.

Northward

I was born a long way from my resources,
pinned in a corner of the South
but the signposts always pointed north.
I followed them, stretching further each time.

Almost there now, I am moving
up and down weekly as a shuttle.
I find myself tilting recklessly
to the northern peak of conversations.
I listen and tune in, cricking my neck.

The North is itself, and nothing more.
So many castles that the enemy still roams,
ghosts of merry dancers in the garrisons,
the surly curtain of coastline
and winds that disentangle the mind.

My dreams become stormy and thirsty;
the spirits of unborn children
dart between heaven and the inferno
then shiver in the water like fish.
I wake with blue salt on my tongue.

I do not know if it's possible to be too far north,
whether the gulls swoop over your sleep,
a huskiness climbs your throat
as you call and call and are not heard.

Letting Her Go

My mother will abandon land,
her three wheelchairs and three hoists.
I'll wrap her in the cream shawl
then lift her into a cave, its roof alive
with lichen and spleenwort fern.
I'll place her on a ledge, and leave.
The tide will come in, bringing
two cow seals with mottled coats, drawn
by the ghost howls of their stillborn,
but instead they'll find a bone-woman
and they'll stretch their crinkled necks
to sing to her in shades of light and dark,
sing her limbs back to life,
while the waves peak and break
until she is silver and streamlined.
The ocean will become her home.
She'll steer through its blue-green rooms
and learn the underwater calls of seals:
the harmonics of their long moans,
the guttural rup with its sharp upsweep,
and the trrot clicking sounds.
When my mother basks on the rocks
after her first sea dance,
her laugh will be one I've never heard in air.

9

Mother and Daughter Seal

It was a rapid birth
on a bed of oarweed along the shoreline.

First you sniffed me seven times;
already you feared the folds of skin
wrinkling my neck and body,
the icy whiteness of it splayed over a rock.

You made strange howls in my direction –
it sounded like the wind calling.
You soon recognised the noises I made in reply,
fathomed my hunger

so big and so bright.
You flippered me up and down
until your soft cream underside became mine.

Mother, I never saw you eating
during the three weeks I feasted off you.
My girth quadrupled in size.
Impossible to believe how quickly I used you up.

You humped your body around,
arms flapping
as if you were drowning on the sand.

There was a restlessness before you went,
as you scratched at the ground and couldn't
scare the gulls off any more.

You gave me everything:
this thick grey coat and all my seal layers.

A Maternal Precaution
after an Orcadian superstition

Before that first sea journey
she painted a cross
over her daughter's breasts,
because you never knew
who or what was waiting
out there behind the islands
where rocks were not always
rocks; one glimpse
of the blood-red strokes
scoring the girl's chest
into quarters would be enough
to ward off even
a muckle selkie-man
and nine months on,
a bairn
with hairy webs
between its fingers and toes,
pads on its palms and soles,
and eyes that had probed
the ocean floor.

The Island's Bride

i The Causeway

The mudflats are breaking out
into a water script,
the tide's last words.

From a peninsula of sand
I appoint myself
interpreter of their sentences,
every twelve hours to unravel a new text.

ii The Refuge Box

One day I'll allow myself
to compete in a race with water.

Here I am in one of the little huts
on stilts, my skirt hitched,
not waiting
for the yellow helicopter,
a north-easterly cajoling me
as I sway and stagger
on my new wooden legs,

then wade out into the beyond.

iii Choices

On the causeway
  between *Pilgrims Way* and *Snook Neck*

   in the Old Ship pub
   between *Buoys* and *Gulls*

    at the village crossroads
    between *Straight* and *Crooked Lonnen*

     along the rocks
     between *Bride's Hole* and *Snipe Point*

      by the empty jetty
      between *Moody* and *Faithful.*

iv *Lindisfarne is more than*

the ghosts of old herring boats
overturned into huts,
with tarred roofs and locked doors;

a castle presiding on a giant spark
of dolerite, like a god
who must be consulted;

a place where stones are spirits
and rocks mount into boulders
that lodge in your throat;

the red walls of the priory
opening to the elements, growing
into a ruin, into itself;

a cemetery for holy corpses
who do not decompose
but seek sleep and refuge;

wind flaming across sand into cliffs,
while coarse grasses run away
or bow in prayer;

the *insula sacra*.

v   Questions

The sea breathes in and out,
heaving nearer each minute, but no-one
will ever measure it, not even
the wave consultant with his instruments.

I imagine him, an aquatic mathematician,
swimming around in his mind
in search of a formula
for the height and weight of water,
though even this would not explain
how a spring tide vibrates
the foundations of a house,
leaving a crack distinct as a voiceprint
down centuries-old sandstone walls,
or how the moon pulls the ocean's reins.

This man paces the foreshore,
listening to his inner rhythm
while the sea brings the same questions
to and fro, spreading them at his feet.

One vast page ranging away from view,
   no paragraphs for pauses. Where to begin,
how to find a loose thread that invites
   unravelling. Each sentence slips out of
its predecessor and into the next, wave
   upon wave of calligraphy, not a lapse or
hesitation in sight. This is a complex
   and perfect grammar, and I always loved
a verb table, the way tenses string
   together as pearls, each mirroring another,
and those cupboards a linguist builds
   in her mind, where accusative, dative,
genitive are stored for instant access,
   the carved drawers of etymology, where
tide derives from *time*. Later, I may
   evolve into marine lexicographer, a creature
of the shore, gathering and annexing
   the sea's textures, until I become bilingual
in its liquid language. But for now
   I must learn the words as a child does,
like braille, tracing them by finger
   in the sand, the slow kinaesthetic method.
My first letter is the shape of a small
   purse, or is it a lip, just slightly open.

How effortless to slip away
as if overwintering here,
then knit and loop myself
into the safe crossing times,

to let the wind crumple me until
I'm an old map, while the tides
nudge the edge of my sleep,

to trace the coast with a fingertip
and witness it go missing
some days behind the haar,

to learn and grow a new language
that only the sea and I
will speak together,

to assign myself the island's bride
and leap over the petting stone.

Lindisfarne is asleep, and at last alone.
Sea has cast it off from the mainland,
swallowed the causeway inch by inch.

The dunes glint, and I spot a ribbon
of unexplored sand to the west.

Layers of cloud, land and ocean
mesmerize me, pierced only
by the tooth of castle on Beblowe Crag.

It is a place adrift, but not drowning.
An afterthought of creation perhaps,
or the first country ever.

I have left a fragment of myself resting
on one of the island's ancient pillowstones.

The Sister

On breaking through the skin of that old dream
where I resit my maths exam, I remember
the sister I never had. We chose her name,
conceived her from a dictionary. Catriona.

A girl born under the potent spell of numbers,
so when she'd counted bottles on a shelf
she'd write the sums all over her pyjamas,
then trot contentedly into night, with proof

that life added up. I picture her aglow
at thirty, beguiled by probability.
She floods her senses in the Poisson Law
of Distribution, tastes the poetry,

each sister guarding her end of the sofa
while integers and images spark together.

The Underwriter

Was my father junior to the writer
or did he add a teacher's grade at the end?

Did he write in invisible ink
so his flourishes became an underlayer

illuminating the real writer,
or were all his lines traced over

until nothing remained of him on the page?
It was a dark trade.

He was always predicting
accidents that failed to happen:

never leave luggage in the hall overnight,
it blocks the exit in case of fire.

In response to our wanting and longing
his favourite word was *No* –

he took measured steps to reach it, as if
those two letters expressed the essence of him.

Even now, when I follow my father
through his faltering script

and lower my eyes into his signature,
I sense another world rippling below,

a village that had minded itself
until swallowed whole by water.

Overnight in my Childhood Home

Why is this bungalow
so full of water washing us
even behind the walls?
The toilet flushes once, twice,
the tanks keep filling.

Silent rivulets of bleach.
Then her slippers shushing
slowly along the hall carpet
as she clings to her trolley,
the shaky squeak of its wheels.

I try to remember the prayer
she used to whisper years ago
when tucking us in –
Jesus, gentle shepherd,
guard thy little lamb tonight …

My mother is sobbing
at the kitchen table. I know
her hands are spread in front of her
as if God must inspect them
before He allows her to sleep.

Bespectacled

Amelia and I often swapped frames
despite warnings we'd both end up
blinder than we were already.
Both of us, squat on the ottoman
goggling out of the window:
a pair of owls behind two panes of glass.

No wonder we saw things others didn't.
When a rainbow arched over us
she identified an eighth layer called *roseate*
and with her glasses on, I swear I spotted it.

Amelia claimed she experienced visions
denied to those with bare faces
so she even hurried to bed in her glasses,
soaring like an aviator into the night.

Two years older, yet she didn't notice
that our eyes had hardened to marbles,
or hear when kids nicknamed us
the bottle bottom sisters.

I vowed to wear mine indoors only
and in the classroom if it was Maths;
blurred words made stories
but blurred numbers caused disaster.
Amelia and school didn't go together:
she read the clouds and wrote over the sky.

We'd passed through all the NHS colours
for girls – pink, white and blue –
until only tortoiseshell remained.
Tired of waving to people I didn't know

I begged for contact lenses,
preparing to spill a year's worth of tears.
I learned how to drop the minuscule dome
over the target of the eyeball, the panic
when it lodged under a lid
and refused to budge, the slow extraction.

On my first stroll as an unbespectacled person
I was dazzled by the serrations of leaves,
the sudden crystallizing
of the world's border.

It was then I left Amelia behind
until she almost disappeared,
as near and far
as an exhibit behind glass.

When a Giant Ages

I used to stare in awe
at my father's wellington boots:
fit for a giant
and swirled with the earth.

Impossible to believe I'd ever
shoot up, become large enough
to fill the unknown
tunnels of those boots.

Once I climbed in,
wondering where they'd take me.
I was rooted to the spot
until he extracted me.

Side by side with his
on the back doorstep
my boots were gleaming red,
a pair of L plates.

*

I allow extra time now
for a short afternoon walk.
He trips climbing a shallow step,
blames its crumbled edge –

I clutch his wrist,
he snatches it back
to brush down his raincoat
then straightens himself up.

His nearly middle-aged daughter
is growing taller.
The click of my black ankle boots
over the shuffle of his rubber soles.

The Queen's Sleep

Nothing shields me from his restlessness,
that nightly tramp into battle.
Dropping into sleep, his hand falls
like a drawbridge over my shoulder.
My body frozen into a stone queen,
head tangled with ladders and tightropes.

I married a man who decrees
there will be a new bed.
An army of craftsmen coil springs
into a tension gauged to him: firm.

One morning I roam
to a chunk of coast with erratic currents.
My feet run away from me,
years of stillness leave me breathless.

I stretch out, as the ocean does,
my spine printing itself on the sea bed.
My hands unclasp into their underwater life
dispersing as seals and whales.
The sand accepts my shape,

the shore offers a long pillow.
Hair blades out, mad as oarweed
while water breaks into caves.
I smell my self.
Lips salted, mouth filling with word-pebbles,
bring   take   come   go

Ridges and hollows, I am the dune.
As the tide withdraws
I dry slowly, undressed to the grains.

The Girl with Silver Hands

after a story from the brothers Grimm

A handless girl with maimed arms can starve.
I strayed one night into a royal orchard
where fruits dangled like jewels.
Tipping back my head, I stole a pear,
ate it straight from the branch.
The juice trickled over my face,
down my shoulders, and I was filled
with the body of its white-green flesh.
As I spirited in and out of trees
the prince was watching from behind a bush.
But I was no robber. He stumbled into love.

*

I never told him the story behind my wounds.
My prince ordered a pair of hands
for me, made to measure.
Two silver birds arrived on a velvet cushion.
I became his bride,
with my engraved veins and wrists
and hands that had been rinsed in moonlight.

*

I clinked around the palace.
My hands formed a crooked tray
but my fingers were as useless
as a bunch of spoons, unable to reach
for the hidden key or unlock doors.

Every polishing removed another layer.
Softer than copper, harder than gold,
they cradled ice and snow without gloves
but I imagined plunging my hands
into fire and melting them down.

Neither do silver hands know
whether a wedding ring is on or off.
I prayed with the rigid wings
of those hands, and longed to learn what
flowed within their hollow.

*

I reflected so much light
but it did not come inside
and spark my heart.
Every press of my husband's hand
left tiny scratches in mine.

He set off to fight a war
in a far corner of the realm.
If there was warmth at the nape of his neck
I could not measure it –
he fell from my grasp.

*

Seven months later my son was born.
I did not allow myself
to touch the whorls of his ears
or the fine down on his head.
I bandaged my fingers
to wipe tears from his face.

Slowly he warmed in my arms.
He never whimpered at the chill
of my hands, but laughed
at the miniature twins he saw in them
and used his spoon
to ring out songs on me.

                    *

My son and I escaped the sparkle
of the palace for a dense forest.
Years began to spread over us
and the trees became our family,
stooping but not in the habit
of counselling or hand-kissing.

While my son was gathering berries one day,
I wrapped my arms around a fir
as if it were a great-grandmother,
rested my cheek on her bark;
I let my skin drink her layers of prayers
until they tingled down my neck.

I heard two thuds from behind her trunk,
flinched at a glimmer of silver on soil.
I unfolded my arms and gazed:
she had restored to me, seamless and whole,
my flesh and bone hands –

I shook them to believe it, stretched one out
to pluck a speedwell, then a lost feather.
My hands relearned the language
of hundreds of finger shapes
and how to clasp what was mine.

*

In the seventh year a traveller
collapsed at the door of our cottage
before he could beg for shelter.
Rivers of grime had dried
in the cracks of his hands
but I remembered their contours.

A prince has a long way to fall.
He no longer knew me, my mild touch,
as I wrapped him up in sleep.
I hurried to the inner chamber,
the drawer where my silver hands
lay preserved, for proof I was his wife.

In their tarnish I discovered
dark, mottled oceans
with islands of light.
I held one in each of my living hands,
dreamed of mending my husband.
I called our son down from the trees.

Last Words

Two of the world's languages die every month.

When the linguist arrived in the village,
armed with her transcribing tools
and hoping to capture a language
on paper, it was already too late:

the last speaker had died hours before.
She just sat at his feet, the sealed
archive of his body. Too late now
to record him talking to his ancestors

or keep vigil, listening to his prayers.
She heard centuries of stories disperse
while verbs ebbed in his chambers.

The last speaker swallowed the eighty-three
consonants that enchanted experts,
and the taste of Ubykh on the tongue.

Learning Greenlandic

Her words were so long
that strangers sank beneath them.
She calmed me as I roamed
the tortured surface of her mother tongue.

Vowels were swallowed, consonants gathered
from deep in the throat.
The only teaching book was in Danish.

The numbers climbed as far as twelve,
then came *passuq* – many.
I immersed myself in that space
as though it were an ocean.

I learned how to pause
in the dark lapses of my memory,
trying to form a superlative, slotting it together.

She tasted the economy of one word;
what I pronounced never turned into speech.
Stories and promises froze in my mouth.

Throughout that first long polar night I listened.
A blanket of ice covered the talk of her people
as if meanings were trapped
behind all the gruelling winters they had lived.

I longed to be one person again,
thinking and speaking in unison
but was unable to translate it to her.

A man might die of exposure in this language.
She advised me to dress in heavy clothing
and prepare myself for a long journey
with her – a red sun for company.

Silk Escape Map

She holds the land of Burma in her hands
as if it were a live creature
sent to preserve her until the end,
and him, prisoner of heat and dust.

After the plainness of wartime material
this silk map spills an amber glow.
She searches for him in its arteries,

samples names on her parched tongue,
Yenangyaung, Taungdwingyi …
drawing closer to him,
to their three days as husband and wife.

That night she prowls enemy lines,
silent map smuggled in a bamboo cane.
The jungle rustles.
Even in her dream she does not know

if she will know the man behind the wire
in order to rescue him – if she can stitch
him back together.
The few words he was allowed to write
were rotting when they reached her;

his spoken words she has concealed
inside her breast, unsoiled by temperature.
She only lets herself listen to them at dawn.

Below the bloodshot eye of the sun
he is a tiny flightless creature.
But the single filament of him, unreeled,
is thousands of miles long.

She imagines a blouse, both warm and cool,
created from a survival kit.
Oceans stream down her arms,
a mountain chain climbs her shoulder.
She will wear him on her skin.

After Vermeer

The Pause
after 'A Lady Writing' by Johannes Vermeer

It is easy to open with his gift.
The ripple of these pearls over the table;
soon they will play music around my neck.
And here is my neatest script:
he will dream of it, I promise him that.

My lips speak silently as I write,
they even press together at the end
of a sentence, and I confess
this returns to me his kiss, just the one,
the impression of it still on my hand.

But the true art of the first letter
is how to hint at love and brush it in
so that it lies behind the writing,
a faint disturbance in the background.

And I know that letters have colours
beyond the flow of black on white.
This one is ultramarine, extracted
from lapis lazuli, with glints of light.

I pause to gaze while my sentences seep
into paper, then I slowly sign
with all that I am.

The Proposal
after 'Young Woman Reading a Letter at an Open Window'
by Johannes Vermeer

Each morning I loop back the crimson curtain
hoping the light will flood in
and illuminate the part of his letter
not yet revealed to me.

So often I have stood here unfolding
then refolding, the letter getting softer.
I read until the words are moving,
then I read the smudges and corrugations.

I am wearing it all away
with my eyes; now they have glimpsed
the underside of a man's script
and they will only plunge deeper.

I remember his eyes are a not-quite-finished blue
with shadows below, because he surveys
the world from a lowered gaze.

The paper is taut in my hands.
I am stretching it to make him last,
bathing in the dabs of light he has granted me.

His letters are surprises that radiate
into bruises. Yellow pools laced with black,
an apple splitting its skin, browning into a mouth.

I sleep with him under my pillow.
Overnight his words become raindrops
and still I have failed
to translate them into a proposal.

I have let him write all over me.

The Rejection
after 'Lady Writing a Letter With Her Maid' by Johannes Vermeer

I used to hide each message
within the bodice of my dress
until it became a heartbeat.
And so he filtered himself across

but when he stood in front of me at last,
all red-black and decorated, I knew
I had viewed him from behind a curtain.
Something toppled inside me.

The pages are still surging
out of him, words bumping together
and penstrokes ever darker:
a woman can drown in that language.

He has delivered the latest one in person.
Cornelia brings it up. She appears
more damp than usual; all that creeping
through night for me – and also for him.

She gazes towards the window.
I hardly need to peep to know
the pale half-disc of his face is waiting
down there. Even his silence is not quiet.

I do not wish to squeeze inside the life
he has in mind, or stay the same size
for ever. Crumpling his letter, I discover
the hard white knot of my fist.

I take a fresh piece of paper.
Light catches the fine line of my quill.

The Interruption
after 'Mistress and Maid' by Johannes Vermeer

I lock all his letters in the linen chest,
the key an anchor around my waist.
The house is dustfree, shutters closed
so I am not distracted from this task.

I spend a long morning alone at the desk,
wrapped in the brilliant yellow gown
of my marriage, as if I am forcing
the sun to shine indoors.

But with *him* I wear midnight blue,
daring the afternoon light to play on me.
Without him my life is half-length
and every word I write reduces me further until

I am down to the last letter.
How to flow on paper without spilling myself?

Lysbet comes through the gloom to deliver
a slip: his new message.
The weight of my secret is in her eyelids.
She is unable to read or write *Goodbye* –
perhaps it is less final to speak it.

I roll the quill in my hand.
Shall I receive him just one more time?
Or send him away,
burn his words, and return to the house
where silence swallows me.

The Homecoming
after 'Woman in Blue Reading a Letter' by Johannes Vermeer

Notice how he sits on that chair
even when he is no longer here.
A quiet man of muted ochre tones,
flat and intricate as a map.

He is forever warning me that letters
may be misdelivered. His always arrive.
The lines rise and fall across my room,
windows seem to fling themselves open.
This letter I read three times,

absorbing it into my skin.
On paper he bestows the jewels
which elude him in speech, yet he fails
to answer the question aching around my neck:

Can a marriage lie unattended for a while,
a string of pearl lights inside a drawer?

When I wedded him, he unfolded me
a little. Now neither of us knows if
I am the woman he keeps leaving behind.

I may still be without child
but have wrapped myself up in the sky,
growing more ruffled on the surface.
When he returns, I will rely on his eye
to blend all the shadows into a whole.

At certain moments I sense our child
just here, a breath of blue
passing through my hands.

The Intrigue

after 'The Love Letter' by Johannes Vermeer

Maria hands me a letter, unaddressed,
though we both know. Passed onto his friend,
then onto her, it is no longer crisp. Inside,
a tide of words to sweep me back and forth.

He always avoids my name, and signs himself
as *C*, a curve clasping me again and again.
He is fond of a riddle
and has taught me how to navigate codes

but he has divided me
into a shadow swimming along an alleyway
and a sharp stroke of light.
Sometimes my brightness splinters

and it is as if I am peering
through a keyhole,
straining to see all of him at once.
A draught laps against my feet.

Maria's smile reminds me
that my parents have already chosen a husband,
a man who is so old he will always know better.
The three of them plotting a safe harbour,

while I want to fling my shoes
and dance on the sea.
Soon I will disappear into mist,
leaving behind only the ripples spun by a ship.

Blue Shadows
after 'Woman with a Ewer' by Johannes Vermeer

After the redness of dawn
has melted away,
the morning light explores
flakes and abrasions on the wall.
I allow it to follow the arc of my arm
and rinse the inner places
water will never reach.
A moment repeats itself indefinitely.
Rooms relax in their shadows,
doors open and close
as if whispering.
Hand on the window,
I am mesmerized
by the geometry of each glass pane:
let these blues filter through white
and crisp planes of linen.
Mine is a pale life of small tasks.
It is not what I had in mind.

The Tall Man

So tall that he must fold
the upper half of his body
to fit the contours of the carriage.

He stoops there, a distorted
question mark, a tube traveller.

*

If he were a statue he'd be carved
out of bubinga wood,
chisel marks left behind,
and painted in diluted colours.

He can't afford to be in fashion:
he slides off the edge of all size charts.
You'd expect his trousers to be too short
but they ripple over his shoes.

*

The tall man moves
with long, slow, spider strides
down the platform, oblivious
to the mad birds of papers and wrappings
which flap against walls.

He's never been a hero.
He won't rescue me or scoop me up
in his arms, and a gust of wind
would blow that stick figure
down the escalator.

*

I rewind him to a tall boy
arranging himself behind a child's desk,
a giraffe on the football field,
all legs and no tactics –

then he's a baby, so long
that visitors insist on measuring him,
and the white layettes knitted
by his grandmothers are redundant.

*

I would be happy to wake up
to his boat feet protruding
from the end of the bed.

My life is small
but I will make room for him.

*

When he speaks to me for the first time
I'll have to crick my neck and lift my face.

He treats language as an endangered species
and his conversation, when it happens,
is lean, to be spread thinly.

He steps into silence
as I would step into a favourite café.

*

It's inevitable that some day he'll tread
on one of the little people below him.

A woman with mulberry toenails hisses
up at him, voice spiralling like a snake.

The tall man recoils.
An uncertain smile in my direction.

Tomorrow I will tuck myself
just inside the door of our carriage,
plant my size three feet and wait.

Lighting the Dark

Drawing nearer
I find myself
in the mirror of his eye:
a doll too small
for anyone to inspect.

I could almost
love that painlessly
reduced version,
framed and rainbowed
by his iris.

The radial muscles,
those feather rods
of grey and gold,
open me in dark
then close me in dazzle.

His light
is not white,
it is a blue
grown from blackness,
composed of a hundred blues,

it is a corridor
where the shadows
unsettle me.
At night I am restless,
pacing below his eyelids.

The Goodbye Timetable

Through the long farewell,
telescoped sentences are swallowed
by the manic whirr of a black board.

Roses can't breathe in cellophane
neither can ironed lives
and folded words in suitcases.

The barrier grows into a frontier
but the waiting train compels
passengers forward in a straight line.

From the carriage door I follow him
waving, withdrawing, waving again.
Our silent parting has lanced me.

To calm my journey northwards,
only a nest of miniature chocolates
and the voluptuous raspberries.

Breakfast crumbs from his mouth
cling around mine.

Fire Child

I thread myself between twin fires,
allowing one breath for the path.
My body is singed and smoked –
still I bathe in ashes and soot.

Other women will bloom into summer,
picking swathes of white hawthorn.
My blossom is the flames.

There is nothing I will not try:
one night I walk barefoot over hot stones,
my arms a cradle.

In the sparks I read stories of miracles.
Gathering the embers
I shape miniature garments,

plump them into sleeping mounds.
The child is a slow-burning blaze
but I am not yet extinguished.
A fireball of gold swirls within me.

Her Pearl

Unborn. He was dredged up
by years of overhoping,
a sea-grown jewel.

She lulled him in her palm,
explored his almost-
but-not-quite face and form.

No word existed for him;
all the names she'd chosen
were longer than his body,

his smell, just out of reach
so she was always sniffing
nothing.

How to separate a droplet
of milk into a quarter –
the terror of drowning him –

her pearl,
his trapped starlight.
A tear froze behind her eye.

Adoption Brochure

Stanislav looks dry and tired
as if stored all four years of his life
on a high, dusty shelf.

A boy of few words
and many shades of grey,
his mouth is small and straight.

Short white hair, black stars for eyes,
he hides away his hands
in the pockets of oversized trousers,

and I want to believe
that a dream and a secret
are clasped in his fists.

He stands between toy pushchairs
which guard him like a set of parents.
A human parcel, unopened.

The Forest

I tried to wrap her up
in a darkness warmer
than her mother's womb
so she'd never leave.
I mustered every root
waved my branches
dimmed my green
to keep her close within.
She didn't listen
to the snap of my twigs
to the woodpecker tapping
the bark of my oldest tree
so that she might hide
in its thundersplit husk.
I plumped my berries
dropped them on her path
let them burst open
in warning.
The red coat and hood
blinded her to danger
and entranced me –
I let her go.
Below last year's leaves
I still possess
the secrets of her footprints
scars on the earth.
Sometimes they deepen
as if she's lost
begging to come back in.

The Wolf's Side of the Story

She took me for a dog
mooching about in the forest
for a morsel of conversation.
The sort who always wants to be friends
with those not of her kind.
She had to restrain herself from stroking
my grey pelt.
Never came close enough to notice
how I'm sparks of silver.
I hadn't eaten for three days and nights
tongue slumped in my throat.
I bolted to that cottage
barely managed to twist my voice
into a squeak
skip through the door on my hind legs.
The ugly grandmother was gristle.
Her nightdress and frilly cap
toned down my nose
perfumed me up:
a disguise I'd use again and again for sure.
The child climbed onto the bed.
A pretty creature, soft as a pat of butter
her words a clear stream flowing over me.
I didn't spill a drop
except her cape over the floor –
a pool of velvet blood.

Red Riding Hood's Sister

When the cloaks were sewn
I chose grey hard as armour
and requested inner pockets.

My sister dazzled us all
with her brightness, her not-knowing.
Her redness began to itch my eyes.
I should've warned her you can't fend off
a wolf by wielding a basket.

I always carried a book,
liked to nibble at theories, chew over
endings without swallowing:
the real story happened afterwards.

I forced myself to face that beast.
In my mind I've spun him a fanciful tale
and dug my teeth into debate with him,
then gazed the long distance down his nose
into his black-amber eyes.

He's opened his mouth a crack,
I've smelled the dungeons in his belly.
Is it fatal to negotiate with a wolf?

At night he slavers outside my door,
my sleep in his grip.
I know he scours dreams
to a clean white finish.

When I wake I am still whole
with my fist lodged in his jaw.

Red Riding Hood's Mother

I schooled her in all the manners
a girl could need:
how to greet the neighbours,
the difference between nice and nosy,
not to risk the twisting path.

That morning I packed the basket
with the compactness of a cottage –
a round fruit cake, a pot of butter,
biscuits crisping, a custard just set –

and warned her. Yet she dawdled
in the forest to gather those daisies
that were found still fresh
sprinkled over the pillow.

But she can't be scolded any more
and she'll never blush
at the woodcutter's son.

I glimpse her in a meadow.
Cloak flickering like a butterfly,
she rarely settles long.
When I try to stroke her, she bruises
and the red rubs off on my hands.

Listen –
for Andrew and Jonathan

if I saw you fly away
in the shape of swans,
silk wings whipping against water,

I'd gather the feathers you shed,
and enter the forest
to search for you day and night.

At seven I was your teacher –
a chalkdust's worth of patience.
Yet I'd make a home among trees,

comb the moss for starwort.
Fingers raw, I'd spin radial petals
into yarn finer than snow.

I'd sew you each a shirt,
stitch by stitch, white on white,
learning tones beyond words.

I'd agree to all the terms
for restoring you to human form.
The sister with a busy voice –

for you I'd remain silent
two years long, not a laugh nor tear,
listening for wing-song in the air.

Come closer, let me fling
these shirts over your backs
so your swan skins fall away.

It's quiet now, and you
have tales of seas and skies to unfold.

An Overflow of Letters
for my mother

a letter to promise I'll keep writing after you've gone

a letter so brazen with all your taboos
   that it'll scandalize you out of death

a letter that records the loss of each of your muscles
   over thirty-seven years

a letter I would have written to you from my pram
   if I could have

a letter in the languages you urged me to learn
   because you didn't speak them yourself

a letter in the silk stitches your mother taught you –
   satin, stem, chain and a cluster of knots

a letter that will burst open like a peony on your lap

a letter ablaze with stars I have tweezered
   out of the north sky

a letter comprising one sentence that would unravel
   into a coastline

a letter so monumental it'll bewilder the neighbours
   when it's hauled out of the lorry

a stained glass letter of illuminated words I have cut out
   with a knife

a lullaby letter for your longest, calmest rest

a letter for the last room, to lie unopened in the hollow
  of your pelvis

The Marathon Runner

She has the pipe cleaner body,
clavicles jutting through skin.
She has the face pinched
tight by lines of endurance,
sweat dotting her forehead.
She has the cracked lips
and must drink when not thirsty,
the injuries that don't resolve.
Her arms are restless
as she flaps against the past,
legs churning the decades,
the teeth of her bones grinding.
It's a long, long route
her body has chosen,
even with scattered bystanders
to will her on with a smile.
It's a haven and a prison:
days of heavy mileage,
days at conversation pace.
She remembers every lap,
every staging post,
never imagined she could last
the distance like this.
There's no sense of when
she'll arrive or where.
In this armchair
by this bed
behind this door
she's been running for three years,
pressing on as if she's the messenger.

Chapel of Rest

I did not know it was possible
for a person to flicker out so slowly,
then over seven days to grow more
dead. It isn't her below the veil,
and can't be anyone else either.

It's my mother and her old body and a corpse.
The candle flame lights her up into a bride
with oil-painting skin that glows.
It should not be touched.

I lean closer to her left eye,
still slightly ajar, with a singed edge
that won't close over the flood of blues behind.

I should have remembered
she never wore lipstick.
This plum-bruise one thins her mouth
to a slit, pressing flat her last message.

Her arms are straight, their work drained out.
I cannot clasp her fingers, so long and fearless
she was once able to extinguish a spark.
I follow the railings of her tiny chest,
stumble at the ruin of her pelvis.

Only now do I see the lid of her coffin
at rest against the wall, a slanting door
to a corridor where the arrows lead towards the fire.

Perhaps they do not go
so far as we who stay, suppose —
                    Emily Dickinson

At first we sense them following that silver line
where sky and sea merge.

Perhaps they run free without their shadows,
watching over us from the height of trees,
able to stop and hold us in their palms.

We listen for them in songs of dropping –
rain and snow, damsons and apples –
and glimpse them beyond our windows,
in those houses on the river's mirror.

We imagine they've become experts on subjects
such as God and Heaven and Time.
Perhaps they've learned their secret name.

They may take flight,
migrating with the urgency of quink geese,
their wings flurrying our smooth day

then they surprise us by forming a quiet
chorus in the breast. Invisible as cilia
in our bronchioles and alveoli
they pulse us forwards.

Or they are reaching out to us
from drawers, in a wave of forgotten gloves,
reminding us of the work of hands.

Little infinite silences.
Perhaps they are between all the words we write.

Heartwood
for Hannah

You introduce me to each tree
with a sweep of your hand,
overflowing with stories:
trees prefer to be planted in threes
because they enjoy one another's company.

We knock on the heartwood
of a cross-section of trunk, giddied by rings.
What are thirty years between us
when a tree lives for five hundred?
Perhaps there is so much time

that I could age into a dendrochronologist
while you might advance to phyllomancy,
divine the future by listening
to the rustle of leaves.

We wander in silence, until we stumble
into a scent of such depth
that it unbalances us and we sniff
high and low through undergrowth,
don't care about puckering our noses.

The lime. In your country, the linden.
We stoop in its pale green bower to drink
the fragrance, agree that it's not too sweet,
but just beyond definition,
and we're almost humming
alongside a bee filling its pollen baskets.

Autumnologist

After a life of winters you left us
on the hottest day – now the longest
summer is ambering and coppering,
a breeze hushing against my bare legs.

*

On the first day of autumn
I have locked myself out. Waiting
for the church clock to strike five,
for the sun to blush and fall,
for the splashes of plane leaves
on this bench to make sense.

*

Slumped on the bench outside the office,
I am draped in the purple cardigan
knitted by my mother, her loops of love
stretching into chimpanzee-sized sleeves.

I fell on the way to school, grazed my knee.
The hymns in assembly slowed down
to a growl, the teachers swayed, all the heads
whirled in a tide, the sticky floor melted.

I am not dead. My friends are relieved.
It's harvest, the baskets are packed,
but my coat is not thickening for winter.

My mother is not strong enough
to come for me; she must stay at home.
She can still climb the stairs, just.

*

Now I do not lose my hold and fall;
I am pruned from your stem.

*

A glut of crab apples, flushed skins
splitting into lips that weep brown.
I have all the time to make jelly
now, but no interest in the harvest.

*

I shall become an autumnologist,
roaming through the orchard of my forties
with wheelbarrow and wellingtons,
my back curving to the earth.

I keep being swept about, ruckled
by the wind. All my plans are octobered.
Friends want to touch my crispness.

Rustling up and down the spectrum
of fall colours, I invent new names;
russet and rufous never satisfied me.

My hands learn to read leaves.
I store them in corners of my home,
stitch them into quilts and gowns
with dappled, overlapping patterns.

Watch me peel away the waxy cuticle,
ease myself into the epidermis
passing like light through flat cells
down into the chloroplasts

where green breaks down under sun.
I travel along rivers of veins, sipping
the last water.

*

Their purpose must be more
than to lounge about on lawns
or gather in forgotten corners
or choke gutters and drains.

Whenever I stir a harmless pile
of leaves, a creature with too many
legs shakes itself, dares to crawl
out and place me under scrutiny.

*

I still kneel by your armchair,
wrap my arms round your shoulders.
It's not empty; it's like embracing
the limp, seeping stem of a daisy.

*

When we scattered you in the soil
centuries of leaves greened into your ceiling,
hedges blackberried against drowsy roses.

The white-grey powder of you, bone and ash,
mingles now with particles of sand and clay.
Rest a while in this upper layer,
listening to the roots as they grow.

I wish you a quiet winter on the hillside,
with footprints of unknown creatures
passing over you in snow, in silence.

Ripe Fruits

Bring me sticks of cinnamon,
its inner bark peeled then rolled
into a quill with fragrant grooves.

Bring me indigo
so I may steep in lightfastness
between blue and violet,

then the persistence of that first
snowdrop forcing its way through earth.

Show me the book opened
in Mary Magdalene's hands, how its words
slow down against her green robe.

A long-toothed comb of antler
carved by the bone worker; watch me
ruffle a storm as I thread it through my hair

and give me a swing that soars
into a boat sailing over the sky.

Grant me a cathedral I can slide
into my mind, resting unanswered questions
against its cool walls

but allow me also a ruin to wander alone in.
And bring me, last of all
the children who have not come.

Let them climb in that tree and sway
from its low branches like ripe fruits.